HOW TO CALL A PASTOR

A CHURCH GUIDE
FOR THE
PASTORAL SELECTION PROCESS

Written and Compiled
by

MARCEL KELLAR
Pastor
Antioch Missionary Baptist Church
2037 Oakwood Avenue
Nashville, Tennessee 37207

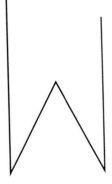

How To Call a Pastor

A Church Guide
for the
Pastoral Selection Process

HOW TO CALL A PASTOR by Rev. Marcel Kellar
Copyright © 2008 by R.H. Boyd Publishing Corporation

6717 Centennial Blvd.
Nashville, TN 37209-1017

ISBN 1-58942-352-6

All Scripture quotations, unless otherwise noted, are taken from the *King James Version* of the Bible, or are the author's paraphrase of it. Scripture passages marked NIV are taken from the Holy Bible, *New International Version*. Copyright © 1973, 1978, 1983 by International Bible Society. Used by permission of Zondervan Publishing House.

Printed in the United States of America

Kellar, Marcel
How To Call A Pastor

TABLE OF CONTENTS

The Parson
†

Wide was his parish, houses far asunder;
Yet none did he fail, in rain or thunder,
In sickness in sin, or any state;
To visit to the farthest, small and great
Going afoot, and in his hand, a stave,
This fine example to his flock he gave
That first he wrought, and afterwards he taught . . .

To lead folk to heaven with fairness
Of good example was his business.
But if some sinful one proved obstinate,
Whether they were of high or low state,
Him he reproved, and sharply, I know
There is nowhere a better priest, I know...

But Christ's own love and His apostles' twelve
He taught, but first he followed it himself.

— The Parson's Portrait,
The Canterbury Tales
by Geoffrey Chaucer

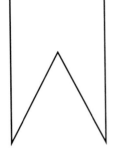

‛Foreword

DR. FORREST E. HARRIS

PRESIDENT, AMERICAN BAPTIST COLLEGE
NASHVILLE, TENNESSEE
DIRECTOR, KELLY MILLER SMITH INSTITUTE ON
BLACK CHURCH STUDIES
VANDERBILT DIVINITY SCHOOL
NASHVILLE, TENNESSEE

The most important process of theological and spiritual discernment a congregation goes through is that of seeking pastoral leadership. Unfortunately, churches often proceed into this process depending only upon traditional ecclesial views of how to call a new pastor; therefore, many churches testify that a maze of confusion develops during the process. Often, the congregation neither theologically understands how to embrace this process nor how it shapes the ministry of the church. The congregational calling of a new pastor does not involve identifying a person with the appropriate gifts, commitments, and skills to spiritually lead a church in ministry. It is a process of discernment that involves raising critical questions regarding the identity of the congregation: Who have we been? Who are we now? and What do we want to become? The response to these questions should align with the faith tradition of the church.

How to Call a Pastor: A Church Guide for the Pastoral Selection Process compiled by Marcel Kellar is a useful tool for this process. I highly recommend it for the advisement and counsel of pulpit search committees as they engage the church in the process of evaluating and defining pastoral leadership.

Introduction

The selection of a pastor is one of the most important events in the life of a Christian congregation. Therefore, care should be taken to remind each parishioner of the seriousness, sacredness, and holiness of the process in which they are about to engage.

An essential committee for the Baptist Church is the Pastoral Search Committee. This committee is a necessary link between the congregation and an organized quest for a new pastor. When a congregation finds itself seeking a new shepherd, it is believed that God chooses a particular person for a particular time and for a particular assignment in the life of each congregation. Therefore, under God's divine plan, the new pastor will help the congregation perfect God's ministry for the edification of the Christian believer unto the glory of God. Due to the shepherd's importance in the church obtaining its earthly goals, the search committee becomes integral to the spiritual health of the congregation. This makes the selection process vital to the survival of each church. Therefore, in light of copious misunderstandings and the lack of specific organized guidelines for the pastoral selection process in many churches, the following document is recommended for congregational consideration and use in the pastoral selection process. The following passages communicate the seriousness of never leading God's children astray and the importance God places on legitimate church leadership.

Jeremiah 3:15, "Then I will give you shepherds after my own heart, who will lead you with knowledge and understanding" (NIV).

Ezekiel 34:23, "I will place over them one shepherd, my servant David, and he will tend them; he will tend them and be their shepherd" (NIV).

Jeremiah 23:1-2, "'Woe to the shepherds who are destroying and scattering the sheep of my pasture!' declares the LORD. ...'Because you have scattered my flock and driven them away and have not bestowed care on them, I will bestow punishment on you for the evil you have done...'"(NIV).

Acts 20:28, "Keep watch over yourselves and all the flock of which the Holy Spirit has made you overseers. Be shepherds of the church of God, which he bought with His own blood" (NIV).

1 Peter 5:2, "Be shepherds of God's flock that is under your care, serving as overseers—not because you must, but because you are willing, as God wants you to be; not greedy for money, but eager to serve" (NIV).

When entering into the process of selecting a pastor, keep in mind there may be a great difference between the pastor that God has called to guide His sheep and the pastor the church wants to hire. Beginning the search process with what God wants is more important than starting it with denominational politics, church constitutions, and bylaws. Consult the Word of God; the Bible provides complete references about the shepherd's call and his responsibility to God and the flock. The God-called and appointed shepherd is *one who cares for the flocks*, Genesis 31:38-40, Psalm 78:52-53, Luke 2:8; *one who defends the flocks*, 1 Samuel 17:34-35; *one who leads the flocks to rest*, Psalm 23, Song of Solomon 1:7, Jeremiah 33:12; *one who is accountable for the flocks*, Leviticus 27:32, Jeremiah 33:13; *one who knows the flocks by their names*, John 10:3-5; *one who keeps the sheep and the goats separate*,

Matthew 25:32; *one who waters the flocks*, Genesis 29:2-10; and *one who keeps the flocks in the folds*, Numbers 32:16, John 10:4.

There is no formula that will guarantee success in the pastoral selection process. However, these suggested principles, procedures, and practices should serve as stable guidelines for congregations in search of a pastor who will lead them in the ways of God. Throughout this process, keep in mind that endurance and faithfulness will be rewarded by God.

I would like to give special thanks to my wife, Lovie, and my co-laborers in ministry for 46 years. I also would like to thank my children and grandchildren who are always there with smiles and a twinkle in their eyes to add encouragement for the task at hand. Thank you, Dr. John G. Corry, Dr. Norman, and Mrs. Mae Reed for your prayers and for your valuable suggestions for the enhancement of this work. Finally, may all be done for the glory of God as we strive to mend broken lives and as the Holy Spirit empowers us to build the kingdom of God in the hearts of all mankind.

Marcel Kellar, Pastor
Antioch Missionary Baptist Church

Dedication

This book is dedicated to my Alma Mater,
The American Baptist College,
the Faculty, and the Student Body

The Birmingham Baptist College

The Interdenominational Ministers' Fellowship
and its presidents:
the late Dr. Andrew L. White
the late Bishop Michael L. Graves
Dr. Dogan Williams, Ret.
Dr. Wallace C. Smith
Dr. Forrest E. Harris
Dr. John G. Corry
Reverend James "Tex" Thomas
Reverend Edwin C. Sanders
Reverend Enoch Fuzz
Bishop George W. Price

and

My very dear friends,
Dr. Norman and Mae Reed

When the Pastor Resigns, Retires, or Expires

E very congregation must deal with the resignation, death, or retirement of their pastors. It is best to always be prepared for the inevitability of these events. And with the mature, spiritual guidance of church leaders, this process can be healing and beneficial to all parties involved. This chapter will help counsel congregations on their journey through this particular segment of church life.

WHEN THE PASTOR RESIGNS

When God sends a pastor to shepherd His sheep, the flock often will look forward to, and sometimes expect, a life-long relationship with this person. However, a single congregation rarely keeps a pastor for the duration of the appointed ministry. There are numerous reasons why God disperses His servants to multiple congregations.

Why do pastors resign?
Resignation occurs for many reasons.
1. God sends His shepherds to serve other pastures.
2. Growth of the kingdom of God (Acts 8:26-40; 13:1-3).
3. For the needs of the pastor and his family (1 Tim. 5:8).
4. When a pastor and a congregation have reached their full growth potential.
5. When there are significant changes in the events of our times.

When the pastor resigns, especially to accept the pulpit of another congregation, there is a feeling of loss, numbness, and anxiety amongst congregational members. These feelings become more of an issue when there has been longevity in the tenure of the pastor. During the incumbency, a pastor who is respected and loved by the congregation may develop deep bonds of mutual trust and love. Unfortunately, this makes the separation process much more difficult for both parties.

On the other hand, members of the congregation sometimes experience feelings of anger, hostility, and ambivalence. For some parishioners, it is as though a family member has died or abandoned them. Unfortunately, there are many examples of offended congregations who punish the exiting pastor by withholding paychecks and other promised benefits. This is often done as a retaliation for perceived abandonment or broken promises. Many times, a congregation may feel that this is the only course of action they may have in order to reinstate their power. This is when a search committee becomes integral to the health of a church. The committee will provide the needed stability and direction that will prevent a church from feeling as if they are powerless. Always keep in mind that if the pastor resigns in good standing with the congregation, then all amenities should be given that were established in the beginning. A mature congregation will have a less painful departure process that instills dignity and a spirit of Christlike love among the members. Therefore, plans should be made to assist the minister and family in whatever manner protocol may dictate. The highlight of such a departure could be a banquet in the pastor's honor with community members and friends celebrating the contributions to the church, community, and denomination.

However, the pastor who is being forced to resign under duress or conduct not becoming of clergy will be far different. This also will make a positive resolution difficult to achieve. There will be resentment from those who have been under the pastor's care, and opposing sides will be created between those who favor keeping the pastor and those who will call for his immediate termination. Regardless of the circumstances, the unfavorable resignation of a pastor will have an impact upon the fellowship of the congregation and the reputation of the pastor. Restraint, coupled with love, becomes the voice of reason and prevents irreparable harm to all parties. Always remember that reconciliation is possible if forgiveness and love are allowed to prevail. Treat the departing shepherd with love, respect, and understanding, and God will bless the congregation.

Unfortunately, a departure of this nature creates a vacuum that is difficult to fill. If the church has elected an assistant pastor who has full pastoral responsibilities in the absence of the pastor, the period of transition will be under the lead minister's leadership. If the congregation consents, then the assistant pastor may be elected to the permanent position of pastor for the church. However, if no assistant pastor has been elected by the church, then strong leadership from the laity will be required to meet the challenges before them. In most cases, this will be the chairperson of the ministry of deacons or the church administrator.

WHEN THE PASTOR RETIRES

When pastors reach a certain age, they can no longer carry the active banner of battle; they are honored to become the Jethros and Deborahs of their age. "Thou shalt rise up before the hoary head, and honour the face of the old man, and fear thy God; I am the LORD" (Lev. 19:32, KJV). They will become the men and women of wisdom who give counsel to those who have the battles of life yet to fight. These men and women are "worthy of double honour" (1 Tim. 5:17, KJV).

The pastor who is departing under these circumstances will always be held in high honor. Everyone will be filled with joy and pleasant memories as the church and its community celebrates the ministry of the shepherd who has served God's glorious Church; therefore, a celebration to honor the pastor's work is appropriate. "Give everyone what you owe him…if respect, then respect; if honor, then honor" (Rom. 13:7, NIV). When the shepherd is revered with high esteem, honor and glory are brought to the realm of God.

WHEN DEATH REMOVES THE PASTOR OF THE CHURCH

The departure of the shepherd from the flock due to death is most painful. The congregation will feel the impact of grief, sorrow, and loss as they wander through the valleys of uncertainty about their future spiritual leadership. The death of their shepherd will provoke many emotions within the congregation, and these emotions may be difficult to overcome. However, through much fervent prayer, patience, and faith, everyone can be healed because the Word of God says that His children are overcomers through His grace.

In considering the final celebration of the pastor's life, please remember personal wishes. With approval of the pastor's family, assist in the planning of a homecoming. Feel free to consult *Boyd's Pastor Manual*, pp. 179-184, regarding questions and concerns for the decisions to be made. Keep the occasion sacred, respectful, and memorable. One final note: make sure the wishes of the pastor's family are given every consideration; this is of paramount importance during this painful process.

There should be a period of mourning as Israel did for Moses (Deut. 34:5-10) and the disciples did for Jesus (Acts 1:1-4). This can be a time for evaluation and reflection upon the teachings of the pastor, especially on how to handle grief and loss. Congregations also can revisit their vision, mission, and ministry; this will keep the church focused and goal-oriented throughout the mourning and searching period.

ONE OTHER CONSIDERATION

If the pastor becomes ill or incapacitated, one important notion to remember is that the congregation should assist in accordance with the church's abilities. Every congregation should be prepared for uncontrollable calamities by planning for unexpected events in the minister's life during the early years of the pastor's tenure.

The Challenge of Opportunity

At the close of a shepherd's ministry with any congregation, many questions will be asked, such as: "What do we do now?"; "Who will be our next pastor?"; "What are the guidelines for such a task?" The challenge will become keeping the sheep in the pasture. When there is no shepherd, sheep tend to meander from pasture to pasture grazing on anything. Without proper guidance, the members of the congregation will take a spiritual hiatus and most will become "laissez-faire" about the important quest of locating God's new shepherd. As a consequence, monetary contributions will suffer due to the decline in attendance, which will make bills and other budgetary goals difficult to maintain.

This will be a great opportunity to provide the church with a time of nurturing a visitation program. Visitation will allow active members a chance to reengage inactive members. Prayer meeting cell groups in the congregation is an excellent opportunity to reach the homebound and those who may live a great distance from the church; this could be in conjunction with Wednesday night prayer meetings and Bible study. The congregation should earnestly pray for God's will to be done in the life of His church and for the coming pastor. Also, the congregation should be directed to pray for peace, unity, and God's abiding love to strengthen the congregation in their journey through the future.

The Pastoral Search Committee

The Pastoral Search Committee also may be known as the Pulpit Committee or Pastoral Selection Committee. This group must be willing to spend a great deal of time in prayer as a group and as individuals. It is important that each member surrender to the Holy Spirit as they lead the church in electing a pastor.

An important question that can contribute to the success or failure of a church's quest for God's minister is the following: How many should be on the Pastoral Search Committee? A good rule of thumb is five to seven and never more than nine; however, this number will depend upon the size of the congregation. The committee should be manageable and represent the composition of the congregation: men, women, youth, and church ministries.

The role this committee will play in the life of the church is of utmost importance. It is imperative that the affiliates who make up this committee be members of the congregation as well as dedicated, committed, mature, and loyal. Remember, everyone's responsibility is to locate the person God has chosen to become the pastor.

ALTERNATE COMMITTEE MEMBERS

Two or three alternates should be elected to serve on the committee in the event of someone's resignation. It would be wise for the alternates to attend the meetings with the active committee but retain no voting privileges. However, the church may choose to elect alternates only when resignations occur.

Notes

Electing the Search Committee

The election process of the search committee usually is only addressed when the pastor leaves. If the previous pastor had a long tenure, then there may only be a few people who remember the electoral process. It is unwise and unprofessional for the departing pastor to make any suggestions regarding the Pastoral Selection Committee.

CONSIDER THE FOLLOWING:

- Will the church's constitution and by-laws be the starting point?
- The church's standing nominating committee may have the responsibility for nominating the Pastoral Search Committee.
- The congregation may choose to elect the Pastoral Selection Committee from the floor; however, recommendations of this procedure is not advised.
- Once the amount of members for the committee has been determined, its composition should be considered. Members should be 18 years or older and proportionately consist of men, women, and youth.
- If the committee number is five, then select two men, two women, and one youth. If the committee number is seven, then select three men, three women, and one youth.
- Voting should be done by secret ballot.

EXAMPLE:

If the nominating committee is composed of five people, then the congregation should vote for two men, two women, and one youth. The ones with the highest number of votes in each category will be selected to serve on the committee. Should a person decline to serve, the person with the next highest number of votes will be asked to serve on the committee. Feel free to adopt or modify this model according to the needs and wishes of the congregation.

Make sure all persons who are elected to serve on the search committee have been contacted before their names are announced or printed in church publications. Once the potential members have been contacted, they will elect a chairperson; therefore, this is not something the congregation has to consider during the process.

Notes

Organize the Committee with Specific Instructions

Most often, the Pastoral Selection Committee has not been provided with instructions of what expectations will be placed upon them. Without this knowledge, the committee will be set up for failure. Remember, it is an honor for the church to ask these members to serve on their behalf; therefore, each position should be treated with utmost respect.

Please consider the following as a guide throughout the entire process. (Each member of the committee should have his or her own manual.)

1. Elect a chairperson who will preside at each meeting, a vice-chairperson who will preside in the absence of the chairperson, and a secretary (preferably the church clerk) who will keep accurate records of all proceedings and deliberations of the committee. The committee should meet each week at a specific time and place.

2. The relationship of this committee should go beyond the formal agreement stage. It is advised that they enter into a covenant with each other to call one another by name in their daily prayers. They should never forget the responsibility that binds them together.

3. There will be difficult tasks within each assignment. However, every problem and issue can be solved with

organization, compliance, leadership, and common sense. "THINK, THEN ACT" is always wise to consider.

4. Each member needs to know and understand his/her responsibilities. Every person should set attainable goals and utilize prayer, an essential tool in developing strategic success.

5. The church's congregation must be prepared to pay expenses incurred by the committee. Therefore, the church and finance committee should approve expenditures. (This should be recorded in church minutes.)

6. Do not discuss the prospective names of pastoral candidates with members of the congregation.

7. All committee decisions, regarding those who will be recommended to the congregation for consideration as pastor, should be done by unanimous vote.

8. Prior to making an offer to any pastoral candidate, make sure the committee has a complete understanding in writing from the finance committee and appropriate church officials regarding salary, housing, fringe benefits (such as insurance and retirement), vacation, and moving expenses. Other ministry related expenses might include books, continuing education, personal computers, and conventions (local and national). All matters should be discussed with the prospective pastor. In some cases, the committee may have the authority to negotiate certain financial adjustments. (This should be in writing.)

DANGER—STOP, LOOK, AND LISTEN!

- The Pastoral Search Committee should never promise the new pastor more than the church has authorized. This is not a good way to start a new relationship between pastor and congregation.

- Do not allow the congregation or the candidate to rush the committee into making any decisions that have not thoroughly been discussed and finalized by the committee.

- Provide monthly progress reports to the church. Without being biased or showing a preference between candidates, members may share their information before the search committee has completed its work.

THE DURATION OR TENURE OF ONE'S CONGREGATIONAL MINISTRY

Most pastors in the Baptist church are called without knowing the length of time they will minister to a church. However, it is accepted that pastors continue in office until: (1) God moves them to another field of service, (2) resignation or retirement, or (3) death. Another more difficult reason for dismissal is due to conduct unbecoming of a minister. This type of situation can be detrimental to the faith and life of a church. Dismissals such as this are determined by a majority vote of the congregation. If there is a reason to sever the relationship between the pastor and congregation, other than death, a 60-day written notice should be presented to the church. It is suggested that a severance package of one month's pay with appropriate amenities be provided for the departing pastor. Keep in mind the admonishment of the apostle Paul, "Let all things be done decently and in order" (1 Cor. 14:40, KJV).

Supplying the Pulpit During the Interim

During the interim period of when a pastor leaves and a new pastor is established, the Pastoral Search Committee must make important decisions concerning preaching assignments. The pulpit should never be without someone to proclaim the Word of God. Also, the importance of not neglecting the interregnum cannot be overstated. The leaders of the congregation may use this time to rethink and reevaluate the ministries of the church by considering how the congregation can reach out and serve the larger community. These are issues that should be discussed as the committee begins to think about the pastoral process and the needs of the congregation during this brief interlude.

TASKS FOR SUPPLYING THE PULPIT DURING THE INTERIM

- The Pastoral Search Committee should develop a current file of available, active, and retired clergy.
- For the first 30 to 45 days, consider members of the church clergy staff as appropriate pastoral alternates. This would also include the period of mourning for a pastor who is deceased (Deut. 34:5-10; Acts 1:1-4).
- If the committee wishes to consider a larger pool of clergy, the local seminary may be an option. If the seminary is of great distance, the cost of travel and housing may be a determining factor.

- Provide the guest speaker with the typical itinerary of the worship service; the committee may send a printed program, give directions to the church, and provide a place of lodging (if applicable). Please include any other information that would be helpful to your guest (which may also include a letter of confirmation).
- The speaker should be given an honorarium plus reimbursement for travel and other related expenses.

THE INTERIM PASTOR

When the church is without a pastor, serious consideration should be given to calling a surrogate pastor.

1. Consider a few of the advantages:
   - The church will know who is supplying the pulpit on a regular basis.
   - There will be consistency of planned preaching during the interim.
   - The interim pastor will be able to give support and encouragement to the ministry of the church.
   - The church will not have to search week to week for someone to supply the pulpit.
   - The adjunct pastor will maintain the congregation's cohesive identity in the role as the undershepherd. Therefore, the search committee can avoid rushing to select a pastor.
2. Is it proper for the provisional pastor to become the church's permanent pastor?
   - This question should be addressed and finalized by the church before the search process begins.
   - The common rule suggests it is best to select the interim pastor from a group of retired clergy or from the academic community who currently are not a part of the active pastorate.
3. There should be a written agreement between the temporary pastor and the church; it should specify responsibilities and amenities, including compensation for services rendered.

4. Tenure for either the pulpit supply ministers or the interim pastor should be discouraged because this is not a healthy relationship for the church. A period of six months would be most appropriate.

5. It is not wise to consider calling a cleric to serve in the office of interregnum if that individual has expressed a desire to become pastor of the church. Without exception, there will be a few members who will pressure the search committee to offer the permanent post of pastor to the provisional cleric before their quest is complete.

CONSIDER THE FOLLOWING CHURCH EXPERIENCE

During the pastoral selection process of one congregation, Dr. William F. Buchanan, pastor of the Fifteenth Avenue Baptist Church, was asked to assist with the supply of pulpit ministers. He was able to adequately stock the pulpit with well-qualified men and women who met the spiritual needs of the congregation.

This level of trust and fellowship between the congregation and Dr. Buchanan made the selection of guest ministers highly successful. By asking for help, this church was able to receive valuable assistance in locating supplemental pastors rather than having to take on the task alone. This story demonstrates that there are many willing to help. Do not forget denominational entities, associations, state conventions, and national conventions. Always keep the lines of communication open with senior ministers of the community because they are a valuable source for referrals.

FINAL HOUSEKEEPING CHORES FOR THE COMMITTEE

- Assign responsibility for invitation of guest ministers.
- Assign responsibility for travel and lodging of guest ministers, including spouse and/or children.
- Assign responsibility for social amenities during the time they are to be guests of the church.
- Make sure all financial matters are prudently managed.

Stay Focused on the Church and Its Ministry

The interim period will bring as many challenges as opportunities. Therefore, it is imperative that the Pastoral Selection Committee and the officers of the church not allow themselves to deviate from their responsibilities. For anyone to understand the seriousness and gravity of the assignment, an understanding of the history and ministry of the church will be required. A brief history of the church would include its date of organization, the organizing pastor, and years of greatest growth or decline (with explanation). Evaluating and understanding the strengths and weaknesses of previous pastors and current ministries of the church also are of utmost importance in order to provide a clear and concise picture of the church's needs.

The following verses indicate the four basic ministries that characterize the life, worship, and work of a church:

1. Preaching   Mark 16:15; Rom. 10:14
2. Teaching   Matt. 28:19; 1 Tim. 3:1-2
3. Evangelism   2 Tim. 4:5; Acts 16:9
4. Stewardship   Mal. 3:10; Luke 12:42

It is important that the committee take into consideration the continuous change in its community. Know the cultural, religious, educational, ethnic, and economic backgrounds of the surrounding population. These diverse forces will make an impact on defining the role and future of the church to its community. The intrinsic question becomes, "How can our congregation meet the challenges before us?" As the church and the search committee consider the person they plan to call as pastor, they should engage in serious dialogue about these concerns.

Notes

_____

_____

_____

_____

_____

_____

_____

_____

_____

_____

_____

_____

_____

_____

_____

_____

_____

_____

_____

_____

_____

_____

_____

What Kind of Pastor Do We Really Need?

The focus of the search committee should not be, "What kind of pastor do we want?" Rather, it must be, "What kind of pastor do we need?" There are as many distinguishing characteristics between pastors as there are with congregations. Not all pastors will excel in every ministry of the church; therefore, where there is a lack in clerical leadership, pray for strength from the laity. The spiritual status of the congregation and the activity of the ministries of the church should be one of the determining factors when considering the pastoral choice.

Consequently, the most important concern of congregations is whether or not the pastor is a strong, evangelical, charismatic leader who stands strong to boldly proclaim the Gospel of Jesus Christ. Subsequently, preaching is a very important part of any worship service. The preacher must understand that the primary purpose of the message is to evangelize, teach, and heal hurting hearts. Because there are a plethora of types of sermons, it is imperative the pastor structure sermons with the following components:

1. Accurately based in Scripture
2. Centered on a subject or theme
3. An introduction
4. One to three points of emphasis

5. An application to modern life scenarios
6. A conclusion

The delivery mode of the sermon will vary from one preacher to another.

- Some preachers deliver their sermons extemporaneously (the most accepted by congregations).
- Some preachers may use a manuscript.
- Some may write their manuscripts but not use them verbatim.
- Others may use note cards.

All of these methods can be used effectively depending upon the comfort level and preference of delivery by the preacher. Do not judge one candidate's style or method of sermon delivery by another. Let God speak through each candidate as He chooses. Allow Him to use the candidate's talents and skills to bring the message that is needed for the congregation. Regardless of the committee's preference or choice, there will be no church growth when the pulpit is weak.

VARIOUS TYPES OF LEADERSHIP STYLES TO EXPLORE
The Leadership Imperative

The search committee is obligated to recommend to the congregation a spiritually-focused and mature person who loves people and desires to follow God's leadership. If these traits dominate the candidate's personality, then everything else will fall in line.

Four basic leadership styles to understand:

- The passive leader goes along with the flow.
- The motivational leader is one who is able to stimulate people to dream and do the impossible.
- The team spirit leader is one who encourages everyone to become involved for the benefit of all.
- The authoritarian leader is one who gives instruction without compromise.

Other considerations for candidates

- Administration skills
- Organizational skills
- Ability to give guidance and counsel
- The candidate's ability to direct expansion
- Educational background and plans for continued education
- Whether or not the person is bi-vocational

Keep in mind, there is no single pastor who will excel in all areas of ministry. Looking for the perfect pastor who embodies all gifts and spiritual perfection will lead to a long, arduous, unsuccessful journey for the congregation. As a result, many members will become exhausted and will suffer many spiritual consequences. Therefore, focus on locating an appropriate match for the church's ministries and congregational needs.

DANGER—STOP, LOOK, AND LISTEN!

- Do not actively attempt to identify the weaknesses of each candidate. The human experience makes it impossible to find perfect people.
- Do not expect a candidate to change him or herself once that person is chosen to be the pastor.
- If the candidate is a solid Bible teacher, do not expect him/her to turn into a fiery evangelist.
- The issue of age should not keep the committee and the church from considering a mature candidate. In recent years, many congregations have become youth-oriented and have denied themselves great blessings of more experienced ministers.
- Likewise, youth should not be a deterrent when searching for the right pastor. Spiritual maturity is much more important than physical age.
- Do not expect a pastor to lead the congregation down paths they do not wish to tread or to teach issues they do not want to learn. The inability to perform

such tasks does not indicate the qualifications of the candidate.

- Do not become mesmerized by the candidate's physical characteristics.

Notes

_____

_____

_____

_____

_____

_____

_____

_____

_____

_____

_____

_____

_____

_____

_____

_____

_____

_____

_____

_____

_____

_____

_____

Compile a List of Ministers to Be Considered

The Pastoral Search Committee will have great latitude in the selection process; however, do not forget there will be recommendations from the congregation.

EXPECTATIONS

It is blasphemous for a congregation to elevate a pastor to the level of a deity. They will need to know the importance of understanding the difference between veneration and respect when it comes to selecting the right person as their spiritual guide. Consider the following questions when compiling a list of possible candidates:

1. Is the candidate a person we can respect as our spiritual leader?
2. Is the candidate a person with a deep and abiding faith in God, a strong prayer life, good study habits, and strong convictions but is willing to listen to another point of view?
3. What kind of example does the candidate set before others, especially children and young people?
4. How does the candidate handle personal financial affairs?
5. What is the candidate's attitude about those who are grieving and visitation of the sick and shut-ins?
6. Does this person have compassion for the unsaved?

7. Does the candidate have a good attitude about physical health?

8. Does the candidate feel a degree of loyalty to the ministry of the church and the denominational work of which the church is a member?

DANGER—STOP, LOOK, AND LISTEN!

There has been a recent trend of making broad changes in the life and ministry of a church. Some may impact the history of the church, while others may impact the ministries of the church. Changing the historic name of a congregation has been one example of these broad changes. Also, many congregations are introducing "youth only" worship services, which actively seek to exclude its senior members. Consequently, these types of practices can be detrimental to the cohesiveness of a congregation. Thus, the ability for a pastor to embody unity is of utmost importance since a pastor's responsibility is to feed, nurture, lead, and unite God's children.

COMPILING THE LIST

When compiling the list of candidates, inform the congregation by preparing a short biographical sketch of each candidate on 5" x 7" index cards with the following information (this form also can be used when asking for referrals from the congregation):

Name:_____

Address:_____

City: _____State: _____ Zip:_____

Tel. (Res./Work/Cell):_____

D.O.B.: _____

Pastoral Status [or student status]: _____

Retirement Status: _____

Sex (Male or Female): _____

When accepting referrals from the congregation, make sure they understand that it will be impossible for each name submitted to be heard. However, ensure the congregation that the committee will select a cross section of people from the submitted names. If the congregation is larger than 300, then ask each department to submit only two names for consideration in order to keep the process manageable. Please include a final date for the submission of names, and the master list should not consist of more than 12 to 15 candidates. Remember, keep the process manageable.

Notes

_____
_____
_____
_____
_____
_____
_____
_____
_____
_____
_____
_____
_____
_____
_____
_____

Narrow the List for Final Consideration

The final list of candidates for a large congregation should consist of no more than seven names; the final list for a smaller congregation should consist of no more than five. Although there may be more qualified candidates, the committee must take care not to overwhelm themselves or their congregation. Prayer and guidance from God's Holy Spirit will ensure that the list is narrowed and manageable for all involved parties (1 Cor. 14:40).

SHOULD A DIVORCED MINISTER BE CONSIDERED FOR THE PASTORATE?

Violation of one's marriage vows breeds mistrust into the most sacred union between two people. When considering the culture in which the Bible was written and the culture in which we currently live, there are few differences between the two. In biblical narratives, many men and women had shades of gray in their lives: "For all have sinned and fall short of the glory of God" (Rom. 3:23, NIV). There are many good men and women who may have failed in a first marriage who would make good undershepherds, and they should be given proper consideration. Therefore, it is always wise to listen before condemning.

However, divorce is not something that should simply be accepted as a way of life. Marriage is a covenant oath between two people who agree to be partners for life and promise to love and protect one another for their entire lives. There are many reasons why couples do not make it in a marriage relationship. Each situation is different and must be judged on its own merit; therefore, God can use a divorced person in the pastoral ministry. All of God's children are entitled to a second chance; this includes ministers. Neither ministers nor laity should make a mockery out of the institution of marriage by continuously divorcing and remarrying because this is a sign of weakness and instability that should not be tolerated. However, always keep an open mind in deliberations, "...If any one of you is without sin, let him be the first to throw a stone..." (John 8:7, NIV).

THE CHALLENGE
Think Outside of the Denominational Box!

Most have been taught to live, believe, and praise by specific denominational beliefs. However, God's love embraces more than basic Baptist beliefs. As the Pastoral Selection Committee creates its master list from which to select candidates for their pastoral consideration, the search committee should consider thinking outside of their denominational box. This will allow them to exhaust all possibilities and acquire the very best candidate. The Great Commission teaches, "Therefore go and make disciples of all nations, baptizing them in the name of the Father and of the Son and of the Holy Spirit, and teaching them to obey everything I have commanded you. And surely I am with you always, to the very end of the age" (Matt. 28:19-20, NIV).

EXAMPLE

There are many opportunities in ministry today. Simply, "open your eyes and look at the fields! They are ripe for harvest" (John 4:35, NIV).

Reverend Mark Stephen Kellar was reared and baptized as a Baptist. After graduating from Morehouse College, he received his master of Divinity degree from Union Theological Seminary in New York. During his matriculation at Union, he served as associate pastor for young adults at the Emmanuel Baptist Church of Brooklyn, New York. He later served as interim pastor of the Beck Memorial Presbyterian Church of the Bronx. The culmination of these experiences was his call to the pastorate of the 300-year-old congregation of The First Reformed Church of Jamaica, New York. (He was the third African American to serve this historic congregation.) The First Reform Church of Jamaica was willing to look beyond their history and denomination to allow God's placement of the pastor they truly needed. They were seeking God's man or woman regardless of denominational affiliation. This did not mean they surrendered basic beliefs or tenets of the faith, but they lifted the veil of denominational dogma in order to get a better view of God's kingdom.

Reaching outside of the box will secure the broadening of spiritual and intellectual horizons. Each believer's mission and purpose is to build the kingdom of God here on earth as the Holy Spirit takes up residence in the hearts of all believers.

It is wise for all students of ministry to prepare themselves for service to God's people wherever there is need and regardless of denomination. Everyone benefits when the denominational box is cast aside. Today, God is calling men and women who will answer His call to spiritually and those who will academically prepare themselves to serve His people beyond the denominational box. May the blessings of Christ be upon them as they render a holistic ministry to the family of God.

Scheduling Preaching Appointments

Scheduling the candidates for preaching appointments is the next phase of the pastoral selection process. When performing this task, the committee should ask the nominees to furnish full résumés with references, academic transcripts, employment history, and predetermined personal information. From this point forward, only serious candidates should be considered. The committee must be willing to be flexible, especially if the candidate is a pastor from another congregation. Keep in mind how one flock may react if another flock is considering their shepherd to be their leader. If possible, try to complete the preaching schedule within a three to six month time frame. This will require trust within the committee and full cooperation from all church leaders and the congregation. This may be a challenge, but with Christ at the center of the deliberations, all things are possible.

In most cases, the committee will invite each candidate to speak before the congregation during the a.m. worship hour. When officially inviting the guest speaker, make sure to include date, time, and location of the church along with a map by AAA or Mapquest. If travel is by air, please have the flight schedule and a designated person meet the guest. Be sure to provide all transportation during his/her stay.

Rural or small congregations may take a more personal approach in housing the guest minister. The pastor and family may stay in a parishioner's home, provided their residence will comfortably accommodate him/her. Whatever the accommodations, make all arrangements ahead of time and maintain organization and hospitality.

In the African-American tradition, there are ministries that have a long history of annual fellowship with other congregations. In order not to prolong the pastoral selection process, it would be wise to work with the selection committee to schedule some of the candidates to preach at these special services. This is not an imperative; it is simply a suggestion.

Notes

_____
_____
_____
_____
_____
_____
_____
_____
_____
_____
_____
_____
_____
_____
_____
_____

The Final Selection for Recommendation

After all candidates have been heard and evaluations have been made, the search committee should narrow the master list to those who will be considered for final recommendation to the church. The final list should be reduced to a number of three candidates for consideration, regardless of the size of the congregation.

NOTIFYING CANDIDATES FOR FINAL CONSIDERATION

First, the committee should review all accumulated data in each candidate's file. Then all church officers, departmental leaders, and auxiliary leaders should consider the committee's selections for final review. Hopefully, the committee, church officers, and departmental and auxiliary leaders will reach a majority or a unanimous conclusion.

Following final review, the committee will notify the candidates who are being selected for final consideration for the pastorate of the church. The committee will determine each candidate's willingness to be given further consideration (requesting their answer in writing is an option). The congregation will then be presented with the committee's final list of candidates.

The candidates who are chosen for final review should be asked to return for a second preaching engagement before the congregation. One of the weaknesses of the pastoral selection process is the attempt to select a pastor from the presentation of one sermon; this especially is true in Baptist churches. Remember, every preacher has one good sermon; therefore, this will be the time to raise a higher standard. Thus, the final candidates should provide a second preaching engagement accompanied by a teaching session in Sunday school or a prayer meeting.

Notes

_____

_____

_____

_____

_____

_____

_____

_____

_____

_____

_____

_____

_____

_____

_____

_____

_____

_____

Visiting and Evaluating the Candidate in a Pastoral Setting

If it is within the congregation's budgetary means, visiting the candidate's current place of ministry will prove most helpful. In this setting, the visiting committee will get a sense of the candidate's leadership skills as worship leader, preacher, and pastor. Visiting the candidate's place of ministry must be handled with diplomacy and proper protocol. Therefore, after the decision has been made and the visiting committee selected, let the candidate know when the visit will occur.

Upon arriving for Sunday morning worship, do not attempt to enter the church unnoticed (sitting in different sections of the sanctuary will not be necessary). The visiting committee should arrive at church on time, enter the sanctuary together, and sit together. Most parishioners will understand the purpose of the visit. At the conclusion of the service, speak with the candidate or share a short conversation with some of the members. Do not overstay the welcome. The committee members' attendance will be as the candidate's guest to worship and observe.

The visiting committee will then return to the church and make their report to the larger committee and congregation. All expenses for this trip should be defrayed from the church treasury. However, some members of the committee may wish to cover their own expenses from the trip as a contribution to the church. If there are budgetary restraints that prohibit a field visit by the search committee, then this will require the congregation's greater trust in the wisdom of the search committee as they are led by the Holy Spirit.

Notes

_____

_____

_____

_____

_____

_____

_____

_____

_____

_____

_____

_____

_____

_____

_____

_____

_____

_____

_____

_____

_____

_____

_____

Factors to Consider During the Selection Process

In some church communities, it has become a common practice to ask final candidates to give consent for a credit check. On the one hand, there are those who say this is a safeguard on behalf of the congregation. On the other hand, some say it is intrusive and violates the candidate's right to privacy. This phenomenon is new to the African-American pastoral selection process and should be given serious consideration before being requested. In the personal opinion of this writer, this practice seems to be a very bad idea.

In understanding the various generations from which many candidates will come, this may be beyond their standards of trust. However, the Pastoral Search Committee should discuss this concern with each candidate. Because of the invasiveness and possible misuse of credit checks, it is best that the committee err on the side of trust rather than caution. Without doubt, this is a serious matter and should prayerfully be considered. Every church has a right to expect its pastor to be a good steward and manage financial affairs with prudence. "If anyone does not know how to manage his own family, how can he take care of God's church?" (1 Tim. 3:5, NIV). However, in the African-American tradition, this has always been a matter of faith and trust between the pastor and the congregation. It is best to continue in the faith tradition of respected forefathers and not submit to these in-credulous times.

Another topic that needs to be cleared is the earliest date the candidate can assume pastoral responsibilities. This needs to be within 90 days of the extended offer. However, remain flexible if the pastor's spouse teaches school, if they have children in school, or if there are other extenuating circumstances.

Notes

Notifying the Congregation

After the final deliberation of the committee has produced a unanimous decision, each family in the church should be notified by mail. A short biographical sketch and photo of each candidate being considered also should be in each mail-out. The following are also some suggestions for the content:

- State these are the candidates recommended by the Pastoral Search Committee to be considered for the pastorate of the church.
- Include date, time, and location within the church where the pastor's election will be held (the church sanctuary, fellowship hall, educational building, etc.).
- The election should be held on a Friday evening or following a Sunday morning worship service in order to accommodate the greatest number of participants. (This is not a hard and fast rule, only a suggestion).

THE PASTORAL ELECTION PROCESS
The Election of Matthias (Acts 1:23-26)

Every member of the committee must read and be familiar with these verses. All the work the committee has done will be in vain if the pastoral vote is not carried out with love, spiritual dignity, and order. It is important that the Holy Spirit be invited to the meeting. God will not bless an endeavor where these principles are not followed. A regional colloquialism best describes this concept: "Don't ask God to bless your mess."

If the church has a constitution and by-laws, they should be used as a guide. It will provide information regarding who, what, when, and how for the voting process. In the absence of a constitution and by-laws, the following model may be a sufficient guide:

- Voting church members should be 18 years or older.
- Decide the number of votes that must be cast by the congregation for a candidate to be declared the elected pastor.
- The date, time, and place of the voting event should be posted on the bulletin board and in the church bulletin for at least two weeks before the date of election.
- Voting by proxy should be determined before the date of the election and verified by the church clerk.
- Personnel who will assist in counting the votes should be made known to members before voting occurs. This will depend upon the size of the congregation and most times, five will be sufficient.
- There are three methods by which votes may be cast:
  1. Prepared ballot
  2. Standing vote
  3. Voice vote (not a good method because it is difficult to determine the number of positive or negative votes)
- It is suggested that a candidate can be elected as pastor of a congregation when 70% or more of the congregational vote has been established. Most pastors may not feel comfortable if they did not receive 70% of the trust of the congregation.
- It may be advisable for a divided congregation to have no more than two candidates presented to the congregation for voting.
- Another model that may be considered is to present each candidate's name for consideration and vote.

It is ironic that presidents of the United States, elected local officials, and pastors of churches can be elected with less than 70% of the vote. However, children in public schools are required to master 70% of their school work before they can pass from one grade to another. There seems to be a disjunct approach to these systems. Therefore, it will be best for the pastor's confidence and the congregation's trust development to follow the 70% rule.

Example:
A congregation has 175 voting members.

Rev. George Marcus	69 votes
Rev. Mary Foss	64 votes
Rev. Ruben Sparks	42 votes
Total number of votes cast	175 votes

Rev. George Marcus has more of the casted votes but not 70%. The votes cast for the other two candidates are larger than the total vote received by Rev. Marcus. This means Rev. Marcus has been elected pastor of a very divided congregation where less than 50% of the total votes went for him. In this case, the congregation can participate in a run-off between the two candidates with the highest number of votes. This will help solidify the choice of the congregation and instill trust and confidence in all parties.

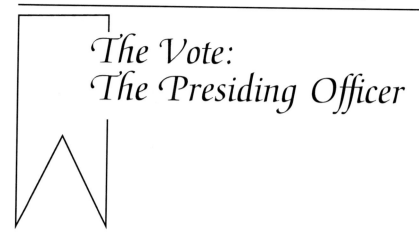

The Vote: The Presiding Officer

W hen the church is active within a local association of churches who have common beliefs and practices, the moderator of the association should be asked to preside over the pastoral selection meetings. Through the office of the church clerk, a request should be made as to the availability of the moderator to conduct the meetings. After the moderator's availability is confirmed, notify him/her by written correspondence 30 days prior to the election.

The correspondence should usually include the following information:

1. The purpose of the meeting
2. Date, time, and place of the meeting
3. Rules for governing the election process
4. Personnel who will assist in counting the votes

It will be the responsibility of the chairperson of the Ministry of Deacons and the Pastoral Search Committee to assist the moderator in maintaining the congregation's order and focus on the objective.

THE AGENDA FOR PASTORAL ELECTION

When the pastoral election has been set by notifying all members of the congregation and the moderator, the election should take place on the date, at the time, and in the place advertised. The election of the pastor is one of the most important participatory acts of any congregation. With this level of trust that God shares with us, we have the responsibility to make sure everything is respectively done with order. At the end of this chapter, there will be an example for the order of the meeting when the congregation is assembled.

COMMITTEE HOUSEKEEPING RESPONSIBILITIES
Ensure the Rules Governing the Meeting Have Been Established

1. Choose a method of voting to be used.
   - By prepared ballot (Make sure there is a ballot for each member of the congregation, by name or assigned church roll number. The name of each candidate should appear on the ballot.)
   - By standing vote
   - By voice vote (Caution is advised.)
2. Guarantee that the method to be used will be finalized before the date of the vote.
3. Ensure that those who are responsible for counting the votes are punctual and present.

It will be wise for any discussions on the candidates' qualifications, strengths, weaknesses, personalities, and theology to be led by departmental leaders. The moderator may allow up to 30 minutes for these deliberations, if needed. Once all questions are answered, the moderator will then call the congregation to order for a vote.

1. If the vote is by ballot, each vote will be passed to the nearest container held by a counter.
2. If the vote is by standing, each aisle will be separately counted in order to obtain a more accurate vote.
3. If the vote is by voice, it will be difficult to get an accurate count.

Proper Order of Events to Ensure an Organized Meeting

1. When the vote has been completed, the committee will retire to a designated room to begin counting.

2. After the votes have been received and counted by the committee, the reports will be given to the moderator, the chairperson for the Ministry of Deacons, the chairperson for the Pastoral Search Committee, and the church clerk.
3. A designated person from the counting committee will present the report to each of the persons as indicated.
4. The moderator will call for a report of the vote from the church clerk to be announced before the assembled congregation.
5. After the church clerk has read the report, the moderator will call for a motion to accept the report; he/she will then declare the vote and report as official.
6. The candidate receiving the majority of the votes or the recommended 70% of the votes will become the officially elected pastor of the church.

Following the election, there should be a reception held in honor of the moderator. This will allow everyone ample opportunity to express their thanks to him/her for presiding over the meeting and keeping everything in order. Also, a proper honorarium should be given to the moderator for expenses. A special thanks should also go to the Pastoral Search Committee for their hard work in a successful conclusion to their task. The church officers should be properly thanked for their assistance in keeping the church focused on their ministries.

The elected candidate may not be everyone's choice. Speak to the congregation about accepting the choice of the majority, and ask everyone to look into their hearts in order to come together as a family in love, peace, and harmony. "...we know that in all things God works for the good of those who love him..." (Rom. 8:28, NIV).

THE AGENDA

Date
Time
(Name of Moderator), Moderator
(Name of Presiding Association), Presiding

Call to Order ....Chairperson, Ministry of Deacons

Congregational Hymn

Scripture

Prayer

Congregational Hymn

Presentation of the
Presiding Moderator.........Chairperson, Ministry of Deacons

Opening Statement/
Adoption Of Agenda ....Presiding Moderator

Reading and Adoption
of Previous Minutes...Church Clerk

Assignment of the Pastoral
Search Committee ....Church Clerk

Presentation of the Pastoral Search
Committee ....Presiding Moderator

The Report of the Pastoral
Search Committee ....Chairperson, Pastoral Search Committee

Open Discussion About Candidates
with Biographical Data in Hand................The Congregation

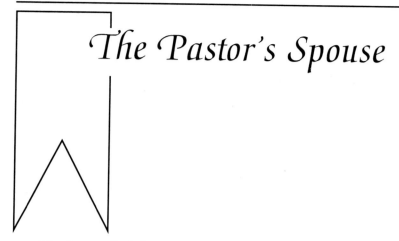

The Pastor's Spouse

*The LORD God formed the man from the dust of the ground
and breathed into his nostrils the breath of life,
and the man became a living being.*

*The LORD God said, "It is not good for the man to be alone.
I will make a helper suitable for him."*

*So the LORD God caused the man to fall into a deep sleep;
and while he was sleeping, he took one of the man's ribs,
and closed up the place with flesh.
Then the LORD God made a woman from the rib he had
taken out of the man,
and he brought her to the man.*

(Gen. 2:7, 18, 21-22, NIV)

The pastor's spouse should be looked upon as one of the most dedicated and steadfast practitioners of the Christian faith. The marriage partner sits among the community of faith in each worship service, gives honor to whom honor is due, and strives to live everyday for the cause of Christ.

When the congregation selects a pastor, many wonder how the talents of the pastor's spouse may be used in the ministries of the church. It is true that when the congregation calls the pastor, they did not call his/her spouse to co-pastor.

This being said, the pastor's spouse should be embraced in the spirit of Christian love as the spouse of the shepherd who will lead. The congregation should always give the pastor's spouse respect, kindness, and love.

SOMETHING TO PONDER

When selecting a pastor, keep in mind that there is no scripture requiring a preacher or pastor to be married. However, the community of faith imposes this culturally-biased edict upon those who are called to become pastors. This is a recent development in the culture of the church, and it may be a result of the Protestant break with the Catholic Church. According to records in the New Testament, the only disciple known to have been married was the apostle Peter (Mark 1:30), neither Philip's daughters nor Lydia were married (Acts 21:8-9). The apostle Paul declares:

> Now to the unmarried and the widows I say: It is good for them to stay unmarried, as I am. But if they cannot control themselves, they should marry, for it is better to marry than to burn with passion (1 Cor. 7:8-9 NIV).

The apostle Paul clearly states that for the sake of the ministry, he wished all clergy would choose to remain celibate; however, if ministers cannot embrace celibacy, it is better for them to marry than burn in their passions. Paul was not calling for the practice of celibacy or the denial of marriage in order to serve Christ, but he was willing to do so for the cause of Christ.

SHOULD THE PASTOR'S SPOUSE BE A MEMBER OF THE CONGREGATION?

At the time of the pastoral interview, this question is not approached for the following reasons:

- When the spouse of the pastor-elect is a member of another congregation, always handle the situation with care and respect.

- As a believer in Christ, the congregational spiritual union to which the significant other belongs should be respected and honored until spiritual feelings lead to change.
- With love and patience, God will add to the congregation as He sees fit.

SHOULD THE PASTOR'S SPOUSE HAVE CONGREGATIONAL RESPONSIBILITIES?

This will depend upon the pastor's spouse's comfort level and the church's needs. For example, throughout one pastor's ministry, his wife equally shared her talents as a music teacher in the public schools and in church congregations. They were accepted as a team within the congregation and the community. Again, it will depend upon the comfort level of the pastor's spouse as well as the needs and comfort levels of the congregation. In whatever area the pastor's spouse can render a positive ministry, acceptance and respect for the companion's calling will further the church's success.

The pastor's spouse is constantly walking a very thin line between not being perceived as pushy or demanding and not becoming a doormat for the congregation. Always show compassion when dealing with a person who lives a life of heightened scrutiny from church members. The congregation's earnest attempt to develop a relationship with the spouse will help acclimate both the pastor and spouse to the new church community. Therefore, the pastor's spouse should be invited for fellowship when the pastor-elect returns for a final interview. This will allow the pastor's mate to get to know the church's leadership and the congregation.

The Congregation's Financial Responsibility

Society has evolved beyond paying the preacher with the harvest from the fields. Thus, each congregation must be willing to accept the responsibility for providing a living wage for their pastor.

If a congregation is following God's rules for giving, 50 members or more can provide a reasonable wage for its minister. However, this calls for their trust to be placed in God and not in themselves. The congregation should keep the following in mind when reviewing and considering the financial needs of its minister each year:

- Size of the family
- Pastor's education; spouse's education
- Local Cost-of-Living Index [COLI] and Cost-of-Living Adjustment [COLA]
- Consumer Price Index [CPI]
- Cost of housing, utilities, and education [children and personal]
- Inflation
- Federal, state, and local taxes

Annually

The following is an example Financial Guide for the Pastoral Search Committee. Actual financial figures for each church will depend on the size of the congregation and its geographical location.

Base Salary per year: This will be determined by educational backgrounds, COLI, COLA, CPI, taxes, inflation, number of children (or intended children), children's needs, and transportation.

Parsonage: This is based on the purchase of a new parsonage at market value and the cost for homeowner's insurance. The payments for the parsonage can be broken into monthly payments via a mortgage, or the church can make an outright purchase. *Or* **Housing Allowance per year:** If the congregation does not decide to purchase a home, a rental property can be used as the parsonage. This allowance should take into account deposits, renter's insurance, moving expenses, security fees, etc.

Utilities Allowance per year: This will be based on which utilities the church financially chooses to support: electricity, water, gas, telephone, Internet access, cable, mobile phone, etc.

Insurance coverage per year: This will be based on the cost of full coverage for health, dental, and life insurance for the pastor, spouse, and children. The church may choose to consider the insurer that currently provides the church's coverage or choose another carrier.

Continuing Education per year: This will be determined if and where the congregation and the pastor decide it is best to attend. This will include tuition and fees, transportation costs, books, other school supplies, computer and accessories, computer programs, graduation fees, etc.

The total salary package will be the sum of all of the above estimates and can be weekly, bi-weekly, or monthly payments per year. (Exceptions include the aggregate purchase of a home and deadline-driven educational expenses.) Another decision to be considered is allocating the pastor a down payment on a home. This will give the pastor as well as the pastor's family a sense of pride, independence, and security. If the church assists in the purchase of the pastor's residence within the community, it can help develop trust between the congregation and the pastor. (The church needs to always remember that the pastor's residence is a house of refuge and should be respected as such.)

Here are some other considerations when determining salary and benefits:

1. Professional Benefits:
   a. Retirement Program: 10%
      i. 5% Pastor
      ii. 5% Church
   b. Family Group Life Insurance: Pastor and Spouse
      In some cases, the pastor-elect may have complete insurance coverage with provision for transfer. If so, the church may consider a shared equity responsibility. When considering insurance responsibility, the age of the candidate may be a point of discussion. This is only a point to consider, rather than a rule.
   c. Hospitalization Insurance: Family Coverage
   d. Extended Care Disability Insurance
   e. Social Security Insurance

2. Non-Salaried Amenities:
   a. Automobile Expenses
   b. Auto Maintenance
      i. Tires
      ii. Annual Tune-Up
   c. Gas Allowance

3. Denominational and Organizational Affiliations:
   a. Association Expenses, State and National Convention Expenses
   b. The Lott Carey Foreign Mission Convention
   c. The National Congress of Black Churchmen
   d. Membership in YMCA
   e. Books and Continuing Education

Another consideration is whether the candidate is a recent graduate (undergrad, graduate school, or seminary) with unretired school financial obligations. The church may wish to consider assisting the candidate with retiring a portion, or all of the outstanding school financial obligations. This offer is contingent upon the candidate being elected pastor of the congregation and should not be considered for anyone who is not officially elected.

Continued Educational Allowance is yet another financial consideration to be discussed. The church should consider assisting the pastor with continued educational and sabbatical leave for study and spiritual renewal.

The considerations mentioned in this guide are parallel to those found in other careers and professions. Embracing these for the greater good of each congregation will reward the church's care and generosity and will enhance their shepherd's service to God.

Notes

_____

_____

_____

_____

_____

_____

_____

_____

_____

_____

_____

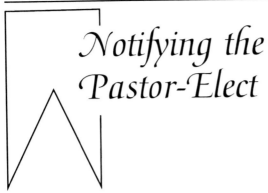

Notifying the Pastor-Elect

When all business matters are completed by the congregation, notify the pastor-elect as soon as possible by either telephone or email. This should be followed by notification via certified mail.

These steps should be followed when communicating with the pastor-elect, the congregation, and all candidates:

1. A note of congratulations
2. The complete vote of yeas and nays
3. The Pastoral Selection Committee chairperson should send written confirmation. Include signatures of committee chairperson, church clerk, and chairperson of Ministry of Deacons.
4. Provide the candidate with a predetermined amount of time to respond to the extended offer and invite the candidate to discuss personal, business, and financial matters for final agreement.
5. The candidate should notify the church of acceptance or rejection within two weeks of this meeting.
6. After all inquiry has been satisfied and agreements reached with all parties, present the pastor-elect to the congregation.
7. The Pastoral Search Committee should notify all candidates via written communication of the congregations choice of pastor and a special thanks from the congregation for their service. If possible, send a souvenir from the church.

Moving the Pastor-Elect to a New Home and Community

There is nothing more rewarding than participating in the process of the selection and election of a shepherd who will teach and lead the people of God. After the pastoral selection process has been completed and all business matters confirmed, the Pastoral Search Committee, in conjunction with the chairman of Ministry of Deacons and trustees, will make recommendations for plans to move the pastor-elect into a new home and community. Whatever the housing agreement, the church parsonage, the housing allowance, or the down payment on the pastor's residence, the committee should secure the pastor's residence for occupancy before arrival.

STOP, LOOK, AND LISTEN!

- The contract for movers should usually be agreed upon with appropriate affixed signatures and all required information.
    1. Date
    2. Time
    3. The pastor's present address
    4. Expected date of arrival

- Upon the pastor's arrival, members of the search committee and other church officers should be the first to meet and welcome the new pastor and family members to their new home.

- A publicity package should be prepared to announce the arrival of the pastor. This would include local papers, state and denominational papers, and appropriate periodicals.
- The pastor's study at the church should be ready for immediate occupancy.
- A welcome reception should be prepared for the new family.
- A congregational housewarming will jump start the process of developing trust, respect, and friendships.

THE COMPLETED TASK

The Pastoral Search Committee's work shall be considered completed upon the arrival of the new pastor and family members. Therefore, the following tasks should be completed before the arrival of the new pastor:

- Make sure all requested personal materials concerning candidates who were not selected are returned to the appropriate persons or destroyed.
- Rejoice and give thanks for the completed task and designate this as a time for the church to pray and ask for keeping the power of Christ (see John 17).
- At the next church conference (or business meeting), the congregation should vote on the status of the Pastoral Search Committee. It is imperative to reach an agreement on its dissolution, unless it is a standing committee by church constitution.
- All members of the congregation should understand that they have a responsibility to themselves and God to assist the new pastor in getting a good start toward building an effective ministry.

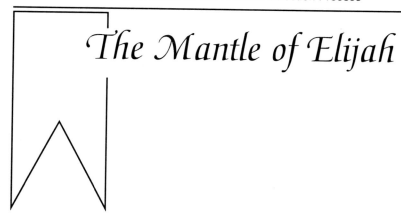

The Mantle of Elijah

The importance of the pastoral selection process cannot be overemphasized. Throughout this treatise, the pastoral selection process has been presented with spiritual and academic integrity. Now, it is time to move the process one step further: the Mantle of Elijah. It is prudent and wise that the congregation prayerfully seek the guidance of the Holy Spirit when considering a policy for pastoral succession. This should be done before a pastor dies or becomes impaired by a physical handicap or terminal illness. Throughout the history of fraternal organizations and religion, the line of succession has always been consecutive.

Elijah and Elisha presented models for consideration. The story of these two prophets is found in 1 Kings 17; 19:19-21 and in 2 Kings 2:11-14. This narrative covers the call of the two men and how Elijah trained Elisha to be his successor. There are also other biblical references to consider:

1. Jesus' successors - the Disciples
   Matt. 10:1; Mark 3:13-19; Luke 9:1
2. Moses' successor - Joshua
   Josh. 1:1-5
3. David's successor - Solomon
   1 Kings 1:32-40; 2:1-4
4. Paul's successors - Timothy, Titus, Silas
   Acts 15:22, 32, 40; 16:2-3, 19, 25; 17:14; 18:5; 2 Cor. 12:18; Gal. 2:3; 1 Tim. 4:6

These biblical references provide illustrations of succession as God instructed Elijah to select Elisha to be his successor. Elisha became Elijah's understudy; this is an appropriate position for any young minister who desires to follow the call of God and have a fruitful ministry. In 1 Kings 19:16, God told Elijah, "...anoint Elisha... to succeed you as prophet" (NIV). Then, Elisha received Elijah's cloak in verse 19.

In 2 Kings 2:9, Elijah asks Elisha, "Tell me, what can I do for you before I am taken from you?" (NIV). Elisha's request was one of great humility, "Let me inherit a double portion of your spirit" (NIV). As the chariot of fire and horses came for Elijah, they were separated; Elijah went up into heaven. Elisha's willingness to follow in Elijah's footsteps made him the ideal candidate for prophetic succession. At the appointed time for Elijah to be taken from him, Elisha was able to pick up his mentor's mantle and become a prophet who was blessed by the Lord.

Today's challenging times require a watchful and keen eye, a compassionate heart, sagacious discernment, and forgiveness undergirded with the Word of God. Every congregation must be prayerful and prudent in their search and deliberations during the pastoral selection process. Thus, if there has been a good relationship between the departing pastor and the parish, then the help of the departing pastor can be invaluable in locating an appropriate successor. The pastor who is spiritually mature and understands the necessity for the congregation to move forward with minimum interruption at the close of the ministerial work can lay the foundation for a successful transition. Similarly, the congregation who receives God's most precious gift of the prophet, the pastor and teacher on whom the mantle of Elijah has fallen, is blessed. There are many examples of the Elijah/Elisha model in today's churches. Here are a few for consideration:

SUCCESSION OF PASTORS

True Light Missionary Baptist Church
Houston, Tex.
Reverend William M. Bowie (Deceased)
1938-1991
Reverend John W. Bowie, Pastor
1992-Present

St. John Institutional Missionary Baptist Church
New Orleans, La.
Reverend Willie J. Hausey, D.D.
1950-1996
Reverend Gene E. Powell
1996-Present

Mt. Sinai Missionary Baptist Church
Houston, Tex.
S. J. Gilbert Sr., D.Min. (Pastor Emeritus)
1964-1995
S. J. Gilbert II, D.Min.
1995-Present

Peoples Missionary Baptist Church
Dallas, Tex.
S. M. Wright Sr., D.D. (Deceased)
1957-1994
S. M. Wright Jr., D.D.
1993-Present

New Covenant Missionary Baptist Church
Chicago, Ill.
Reverend Elijah Thurston
1934-1968
Reverend John Lee Thurston
1968-1979

Dr. Stephen J. Thurston, Pastor
1979-Present
(This ministry now enters the fourth generation.)

Bethel African Methodist Episcopal Church
Baltimore, Md.
Bishop Frank Madison Reid, Sr. (Deceased)
61st Consecrated AME Bishop
1940-1962
Bishop Frank Madison Reid, Jr. (Deceased)
94th Consecrated AME Bishop
1962-1979
Dr. Frank Madison Reid, III, D.Min.
1979-Present
(This information furnished by Dr. Jayme C. Williams,
Retired General Officer AME Church.)

The Temple Church
Nashville, Tenn.
Bishop Michael L. Graves, D.Min. (Deceased)
1977-2004
Darrell Drumwright, D.Min., Senior Pastor
2004-Present

First Baptist Church South Inglewood
Nashville, Tenn.
Reverend Thomas E. Sweeney (Deceased)
1960-1996
Reverend Henry K. Smith, Jr.
1996-Present

Howard Chapel Missionary Baptist Church
Goodlettsville, Tenn.
Reverend Robert McCullough (Deceased)
1974-2004

Reverend Patrick Stanton
2004-Present

The Light of the World Christian Church
(Disciples of Christ)
Indianapolis, Ind.
Reverend Robert H. Peoples, D.D. (Deceased)
1943-1969
Bishop T. Garrott Benjamin, D.Min.
1969-Present
(This information furnished by Dr. Norman Reed,
Disciples of Christ.)

CO-PASTORS

Allen Temple Baptist Church
Oakland, Calif.
Alfred J. Smith, D.Min., Senior Pastor
J. Alfred Smith Jr., D.Min., Co-Pastor

Mt. Calvary Missionary Baptist Church
Nashville, Tenn.
Reverend Willie Russell, Senior Pastor
1977-Present
Reverend Sandy McLain, Co-Pastor

The ministries of those acknowledged in this section are mentioned with fondness and respect. Their dedication to the labor to which they have been summoned should be remembered as lives that have aspired to be like Elijah and Elisha. How blessed are they on whom the mantle of Elijah has fallen.

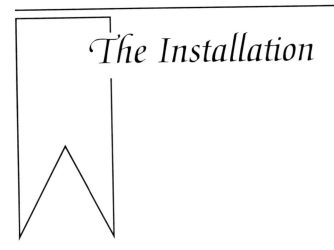

The Installation

The Installation Service should be a joyous occasion for the pastor, the congregation, and the community. This service reflects the dedication and willingness of the pastor and the people to carry out the ministry of our Lord Jesus Christ. In essence, the installation service becomes a covenant between a pastor and the congregation.

The Happy Valley
Missionary Baptist Church
Foot Hill, Tennessee

The Installation Service
for
Reverend Paul J. Mark

THE HAPPY VALLEY MISSIONARY BAPTIST CHURCH
FOOT HILL, TENNESSEE

THE INSTALLATION SERVICE
FOR
REVEREND PAUL J. MARK
REVEREND ALFRED MOSES, PRESIDING

Organ Prelude	Organist
Processional	Choirs
Music	Sanctuary Choir
Scripture Reading: Old Testament	Minister
New Testament	Layperson
Invocation	Minister
Doxology	The Congregation
Music	Sanctuary Choir
Welcome	Presiding Officer

Greetings:

On Behalf of the City

On Behalf of Community Organizations

On Behalf of the Fraternity or Sorority

Special Music

Greetings Continued:
    On Behalf of Home Church
    On Behalf of the Pastor as a Student
    On Behalf of Former Church

Special Music

Greetings Continued:
    On Behalf of Minister's Alliance
    On Behalf of the Baptist District Association
    On Behalf of the Baptist State Convention
    On Behalf of the National Baptist Convention

Music   Choir & Congregation

Introduction of Speaker

Installation Sermon

The Invitation of Christian Discipleship

The Hymn of Invitation

Statement to Congregation   The Installation Chairperson
                                or Chairperson of Deacons

Call to Ministry

ACCEPTANCE BY THE MINISTER

In accepting the call issued by the _____ Church and acknowledging your willingness to serve God as pastor and teacher of our congregation, do you now publicly affirm your acceptance to that office?

I do.

Charge to the Church.

ACCEPTANCE BY THE CONGREGATION

Will the members of the fellowship of the _____ _____ Church rise and make their affirmation of the minister whom God has given them?

Beloved, in the name of the Lord Jesus Christ, do you receive God's servant, the Reverend _____ , to be your pastor and teacher?

In the Lord's name we receive God's servant. We promise and pledge our encouragement, prayers, participation, and labor as we do the work of the Church together. We promise to furnish such financial and personal support that will enable the pastor to do God's work joyfully and productively, as long as our pastoral relationship continues.

The Lord bless you and pour out His Spirit to strengthen you that you may keep these vows in the name of Christ and to His Glory. Amen.

Charge to the pastor.

DECLARATION OF INSTALLATION

In the name of and by the authority of the _____ _____ , I now declare that the pastoral relationship between the Reverend _____ and the _____ Church is now fully constituted. The Reverend _____ is now the lawfully installed pastor and teacher of this church. Let us now ask God's blessings upon the same.

Prayer for Grace

Let us pray:

Lord be merciful unto us. We ask for Your continued strength to render the service whereunto we have been called. We pray for grace and strength for our pastor, the Reverend _____, may Your Holy Spirit fill the ministry to which You have chosen and called Your servant. Amen.

Prayer of Installation
The Offering
The Offertory Chant
The Investiture
The Bible
The Robe
The Keys
Presentation of Gifts
The Right Hand of Fellowship   Officers of the Church,
                                       Congregation & Guests
Presentation of the Pastor
Benediction
      *Reception Immediately Following Benediction

(Please feel free to alter or modify this service according to the wishes of the pastor and congregation or in accordance with denominational polity.)

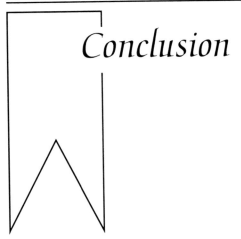

Conclusion

Throughout the years of my ministry, I have watched the inadequacies of the pastoral selection process with a tearful soul, especially in the Black church. The choice of a flawed process or the use of material that did not validate the minister's and church's communion seemed to be the culprit. Therefore, it is my hope that this manual will serve as a guide to the congregation and the Pastoral Selection Committee as they allow the Holy Spirit to do His work through them. Remember, in all that you do, do it unto the glory of God. It is important to remember that the church's messenger is God's angel to His people, and the appropriate preacher, master teacher, and theologian is always sent. The pastor-elect will lead by life's refreshing waters and will make daily intercessions on the flock's behalf at the throne of God.

May every pastor remember the challenge of Christ to Peter, "...Feed my lambs...Take care of my sheep...Feed my sheep..." (John 21:15-17, NIV). When congregations and shepherds practice these principles, they will thrive and grow together unto the honor and glory of God. As the Pastoral Selection Committee concludes its search, it is not a time for them to retire from ministry. Those whom Christ calls to be disciples, He sends forth again and again into the vineyard to make more disciples! May our response be, "...Here am I. Send me!" (Isa. 6:8, NIV).

APPENDICES

APPENDIX I

CONGREGATIONAL INTERVIEW

It will be most helpful if there is a session where a healthy exchange of ideas, questions, and free discussion between the candidate and the committee can occur. In some cases an open discussion forum between the candidate and the congregation is appropriate. I would like to suggest the following questions for interviews and discussions:

1. Tell us about your conversion.

2. Tell us about your call to the Christian ministry.

3. What is your belief about the Bible as the Word of God?

4. How much time should a minister spend in sermon preparation?

5. What is your view of a total church ministry (short)?

6. What is your position on female clergy?

7. How can the traditional church meet the challenge of the current church age?

8. What is your attitude toward Christian education?

9. How do you see a pastor's relationship between deacons, trustees, church staff, and department leaders in the ministry of the church?

10. List three strengths and three weaknesses of your work.

11. How do your spouse and children view your ministry?

12. What ministry does your spouse have that is separate from your work?

13. If you care to talk about your children, what are some of their interests or goals?

APPENDIX II

PASTOR'S PERSONNEL SURVEY DATA

This information will give the committee and the congregation an overview of the candidate's qualifications and pastoral experience. It will clarify the candidates past as everyone works together in selecting the best candidate for service. (Please pass this survey out to every member, and have it returned the following Sunday. This should be done at the beginning of the pastoral selection process.)

1. How much pastoral experience should the new pastor have?
    ___ 3-5 years
    ___ 7 years or more
    ___ Depends on overall evaluation

2. Age should not be a determining factor in the pastoral selection. However, is there an age that the church would prefer?
    ___ 21-30
    ___ 31-45
    ___ 46-up
    ___ Does not matter

3. Educational Qualifications
    ___ High school graduate
    ___ Bible college or college/university
    ___ Seminary

4. The pastor's responsibilities are many. Please indicate in numerical order the five most important to you.
    ___ Preaching ability
    ___ Counseling
    ___ Personal evangelism
    ___ Administrative ability
    ___ Personal Bible study and prayer

___ Visiting the sick and shut-ins
___ Community and civic affairs
___ Denominational affiliations [Association, State, and National Conventions]
___ Promoting the ministries of the church

5. Please write, in 50 words or less, the most important qualities our pastor should have. Please express your honest opinion.

APPENDIX III

SEARCH COMMITTEE'S REFERRAL QUESTIONNAIRE

1. How long and in what capacity have you known the candidate?

   _____

   _____

   _____

2. Give any information concerning home conditions and family background that bears upon the candidate's suitability for pastoral service.

   _____

   _____

   _____

3. What do you know of the candidate's devotional life?

   _____

   _____

   _____

4. What kind of regular Christian work has the candidate done? Please indicate, if known, length of time engaged in the work:

   ❏ Pastorate _____ ❏ Bible class work _____

   ❏ Youth Pastor _____ ❏ Children's work _____

   ❏ Personal work _____ ❏ Hospital or
   prison work _____

   ❏ Open air work _____ ❏ Other _____

   ❏ Evangelist _____

5. Is the candidate continuing to grow in grace, and are there marks of spiritual maturity?

   _____

   _____

   _____

6. Is the candidate discreet in relationships with the opposite sex?

_____

_____

_____

7. Please rate the candidate with respect to each of the characteristics listed. In the space, briefly describe specific instances that support your judgment. Do not check items about which you feel uncertain or have had no opportunity to observe.

(a) Physical condition
  _____ Frequently incapacitated
  _____ Somewhat below par
  _____ Fairly healthy
  _____ Good health
  _____ Health conscious

(b) Personality/Charisma
  _____ Avoided by others
  _____ Tolerated by others
  _____ Liked by others
  _____ Well liked by others
  _____ Sought by others

(c) Intelligence
  _____ Learns and thinks slowly
  _____ Average mental ability
  _____ Alert: has a good mind
  _____ Brilliant: exceptional capacity

(d) Ability to formulate, execute, and carry plans to conclusion
  _____ Does only what is assigned
  _____ Starts but does not finish
  _____ Meets average expectations
  _____ Resourceful and effective
  _____ Superior creative ability

(e) Leadership (Ability to inspire others and maintain their confidence)

____ Makes no effort to lead

____ Tries but lacks ability

____ Has some leadership promise

____ Good leadership ability

____ Exceptional ability to lead

(f) Teamwork

____ Frequently causes friction

____ Prefers to work alone

____ Usually cooperative

____ Able to work with different personalities

____ Most effective in teamwork

(g) Discernment

____ Slow to sense how others feel

____ Understanding and thoughtful

____ Responds with exceptional insight and consideration

(h) Emotional Balance

____ Somewhat overemotional

____ Inclined to be apathetic

____ Usually well-balanced

____ Well-balanced and controlled

____ Maintains balance and control under most difficult circumstances

(i) Willingness to serve

____ Reluctant to serve

____ Motives confused

____ Usually willing to serve

____ Eager to serve as needed

____ Devoted to service of others

(j) Perseverance

____ Gives up easily

____ Discouraged by difficulty or opposition

____ Needs encouragement to continue

____ Capable of enduring to a conclusion

(k) Humility
    ____ Proud of achievements
    ____ Self-confident
    ____ Inferiority complex
    ____ Modest estimate of self
(l) Wisdom in use of money
    ____ Miser
    ____ Careless
    ____ Extravagant
    ____ Careful

Comments: _____

_____

_____

8. Listed below are some of the tendencies that, if present, may reduce the effectiveness of a pastor's work and witness. Underline any characteristics or traits which you have noted in the candidate.

Impatient, intolerant, argumentative, domineering, sullen, conceited, or critical.

Easily embarrassed, offended, discouraged, depressed, or irritated.

Frequently worried, anxious, nervous, or tense.

Prejudiced toward groups, races, or nationalities.

Gravitates toward exclusive and absorbing friendships, e.g., "crushes."

Lacking in humor or inability to take a joke.

9. Please truthfully state your opinion of the candidate's all-around fitness for pastoral service, adding significant information and impressions that have not been brought out by the preceding questions.

_____

_____

_____

_____

_____

10. List other persons qualified to give a sound appraisal of the candidate. PLEASE PRINT.

Name: _____

Mailing Address: _____

City: _____ State: _____ Zip: _____

Telephone: _____

E-mail address: _____

Other Comments: _____

_____

_____

_____

_____

_____

Signature: _____

Title: _____

Date: _____

APPENDIX IV

PASTOR'S CONGREGATIONAL INQUIRY

Questions the pastor-elect may wish to ask the committee and/or congregation.

1. Would the church share a short historical overview?

2. How unified is the lay leadership and the congregation at large, and what were their relationships with previous pastors?

3. According to Scripture, what is the purpose of the Ministry of Deacons, and how is this ministry perfected in your congregation?

4. How many deacons and trustees do you have, and what is the congregation's expectations of them?

5. Under what conditions did the previous pastor leave the congregation?

6. As pastor, do I have the freedom to preach as God and the Holy Spirit may direct?

7. How does the church view the work of the pastor?

8. What denominational programs does the church support?

9. How strong are the following programs of the church:
   • Evangelism
   • Christian Education
   • Youth Activities
   • Missions
   • Community Social Action

10. Does the church hold memberships in the following organizations:
    - NAACP
    - Urban League
    - Chamber of Commerce [General & African-American]

11. What plans does the church have for spiritual and physical growth?

12. What would you consider the strongest ministry in the church?

13. What ministry in your church needs the greatest attention and improvement?

14. What would you consider the greatest event celebrated in the life of the church within the last 10 years?

15. What has been the church budget for the past five years?

16. Does the church have debts? If so, what are the plans for retiring them?

Comments:

_____

_____

_____

_____

_____

_____

_____

APPENDIX V

CHURCH ADMINISTRATIVE QUESTIONNAIRE

1. Does your church year begin with the ecclesiastical year, December to November or the calendar year, January to December? _____

2. What is the size of the active church membership, and how many attend Sunday worship? At what level do they participate in other church activities?_____

3. What method of giving does the church use to reach its budget? What about plus giving?_____

4. How does the church acquire assets beyond tithes and offerings, such as land acquisition and financial investments? _____

5. How many auxiliaries are there in the church, and how do they assist in carrying out the mission of the church? _____

6. How many treasuries does the church have? _____ If auxiliaries have treasuries, how do they use them?

7. How many signatures are required for church checks to be honored by the bank and other business vendors? _____ Is it necessary for the pastor to affix a signature along with other designated church personnel? _____

8. How often are the church financial records audited?

   _____

   _____

9. What special events does your church observe during the calendar year? _____

   _____

10. How does the church support the following ministries: Home Missions, Foreign Mission, Christian Education, and Benevolence? _____

    _____

    _____

    _____

11. What provisions have been made for the participation of children and young people in the life of the church, and what part do they play in the regular worship service? _____

    _____

    _____

12. How active is your church in the civic affairs of the community? _____

    _____

    _____

13. How are persons from other denominations received as members into this congregation?_____

    _____

14. To what extent is your congregation involved in the work of the denomination?

The District Association: _____

The State Convention: _____

The National Convention: _____

15. What physical and financial provisions are made for the pastor to attend the sessions and take part in the work of the Association, the State Convention, and the National Convention? _____

_____

_____

16. Financially, do you support higher education, the UNCF, and the alma mater of your pastor? _____

_____

17. What is the congregation's biblical and theological views concerning female clergy? _____

_____

_____

Notes

_____

_____

_____

_____

_____

_____

_____

_____

_____

_____

_____

_____

_____

_____

_____

_____

APPENDIX VI

A CHARGE TO A PASTOR FOR HIS MINISTRY: TO MY SON, REVEREND MARK STEPHEN KELLAR, SUNDAY, MARCH 10, 2002

To our presiding officer, Reverend Dr. Glen Missick, the Consistory of the First Reformed Church and the congregations who make up the Classics of Jamaica. Today, it is with joy and great expectation that we, the Kellar family, have come to share in the installation service of the 23rd pastor of the Reformed Church of Jamaica. He is the third Pastor of African-American descent to pastor this great church, and is also our son, Reverend Mark Stephen Kellar.

To Mark, my son, I have not come with a liturgy for the installation of clergy to the pastoral ministry that may be found among the writings of our church dogma, but I am speaking to you from the heart of a father to the heart of a son.

First, I will let the Word of God speak to us all through the Apostle Paul's letter to his son Timothy, which can be found in 2 Timothy 2—4 of the *New International Version*.

To Mark, my beloved son, be strong in the grace and hope that is in our Lord and Savior Jesus Christ. Mark, you know my life and the standards that your mother and I have set before you, your brothers, sisters, and our grandchildren. Therefore, I now charge you before God, Jesus Christ, and these people who make up the congregation of the First Reformed Church of Jamaica, "Preach the Word; be prepared in season and out of season; correct, rebuke and encourage— with great patience and careful instruction" (2 Tim. 4:2, NIV).

"For the time will come when men will not put up with sound doctrine. Instead, to suit their own desires, they will gather around them a great number of teachers to say what their itching ears want to hear. They will turn their ears away from the truth and turn aside to myths. But you, keep your head in all situations, endure hardship, do the work of an evangelist, discharge all the duties of your ministry" (2 Tim. 4:3-5, NIV).

Mark, my son, I have somewhat of an advantage over the Apostle Paul. You see, Timothy was not Paul's biological son, but you are the son of your mother Lovie and me. Mark, you are flesh of our flesh and bone of our bone. Today, we come not alone because today I bring with me your grandfathers: the late Harvey Lee Kellar, a trustee of the Mt. Nebo Baptist Church, and the late Pleas Gooch, a deacon of the Mt. Gilead Baptist Church for over forty years. Mark, I also bring your grandmothers, the late Bessie Gooch, Cleora Kellar, and your Aunt Tine. They are here, as they are numbered among that great cloud of witnesses of whom our brother, the Apostle Paul, speaks. Mark, your brothers Gary and Jeff; your sisters Sheila, Mary, and Pam; your nephews Johnathan and Davin; and your niece Maris are all here to wish you, and the First Reformed Church of Jamaica, God's best.

Mark, you have been blessed with a good education and good friends like the Reverends Victor Singletary, Ivan Pitts, and many others. The Reverend Anthony Trufaunt and the Emmanuel Church have been there for you in all things to help you create a solid ministry. Now, God and your family expect no less than the best in all that you do.

Now, let us hear the conclusion of this matter. Mark, we, the Consistory of the First Reformed Church of Jamaica and the Classics of Jamaica are here today to publicly confirm you to the office of pastor to which you have been called. However, we are without power to give unto you the authority of the office of pastor, not even your training at Morehouse College and Union Seminary can do this for you. The authority of the office of pastor is something you must earn through a sincere relationship with God. With knees that are bent in prayer, outstretched arms that are lifted unto the throne of the Good Shepherd, and with commitment to the flock as they give you their love and trust, you will grow into the spiritual leader that you were predestined to become.

I bring you a gift of scrolls from my library of life...take these scrolls, study them, and use them as benchmarks in your ministry. Finally, Mark, my son, remember the great charge of the Holy Spirit, "Keep watch over yourselves and all the flock of which the Holy Spirit has made you overseer" (Acts 20:28, NIV).

God has called you to be a shepherd of believers who worship here at the First Reformed Church of Jamaica. Be blessed, my son; for I now leave you in the hands of God our Father, Jesus Christ our Brother, and the Holy Spirit our Supreme Guide and Comforter.

Finally, whatever things are true, noble, just, pure, lovely, and of good report, find the virtue within them and give God the praise. All things are possible through Christ Jesus our Lord. Mark, I repeat the closing of the sermon of the morning. This ministry is not about you. First Reformed, this ministry is not about you. It is about Him, the Antecedent, Jesus Christ, the Son of the Living God. Amen.

Your father,
Marcel Kellar

APPENDIX VII

SUCCESSION PLAN HELPS CONGREGATIONS STAY THE COURSE

By Jeannine F. Hunter, Staff Writer
The Tennessean

In Jewish and Christian holy texts, the prophet Elijah anointed a younger attendant, Elisha, as his successor.

For years, the younger disciple observed and worked alongside Elijah before Elijah ascended into heaven, according to Judaic and Christian teachings. As Elisha became a prophet in his own right, he sought "a double portion" of the older prophet's spirit before serving as prophet in Israel more than 2,900 years ago, according to *2 Kings 5:8*.

When a minister leaves, congregations often experience a large lag time before a new leader is chosen. In the interim, problems can ensue. Membership may plummet.

But the transition is made easier when leaders have a succession plan in place long before they leave. This is especially important when members or a board of elders play chief roles running the church, as they often do in independent, interdenominational churches, Churches of Christ and National Baptist Convention, USA, Inc. congregations.

The Rev. Willie Russell, 65, senior pastor of Mount Calvary Baptist Church in Madison, loves being a minister and loves his church. Right now, he's sharing the decision-making duties for his 700-member church with his son, the Rev. Sandy McClain, 39. Two months ago, the church approved McClain as an associate pastor.

"A couple of weeks ago, people were talking about me being sick and wondering if I was leaving," Russell said with a laugh.

"I was sick, but it wasn't like I had to go lie down for days or weeks on end."

Russell, ordained more than 30 years ago, values having the time to mentor his son, who once served as pastor at First Baptist Church of Hopewell in Old Hickory. McClain, ordained two years ago, is a father and husband and owns a credit card processing company.

"Is there a cutoff age for ministers to step down? For me, no, there isn't," said the 65-year-old minister, with a hearty laugh. "I asked my wife to watch me and tell me if I am getting to where I am losing it. We all have to go through that; we all have to be watchful for the time when we can no longer work like we used to. I feel I can lift one side of a mountain, but you don't know about tomorrow. I feel good. I feel good about life, about my family and my relationship with the church and with God."

What has his father taught him about being a minister? Being there and demonstrating servant-leadership, McClain said in a separate interview.

"He is imparting so many things on me, and he doesn't even realize it. It is more like life issues that he teaches through stories. There's always a lesson, and it's profound. I look at him and he's not just my father, he's my pastor. He is a very humble man, and God is teaching me humility by watching his servant."

Different Approaches

It's pretty rare in Southern Baptist life for a pastor to name his successor, but it has happened said the Rev. Gene Mims, interim pastor a Judson Baptist Church, his ninth interim pastorate in the Nashville area.

"Generally, Southern Baptists feel that's not a pastor's duty or prerogative," he said. "And most pastors don't like to do that because they are afraid if the guy doesn't work out, they may have interfered where they shouldn't have."

Church constitutions outline the search process. While they vary among congregations, most constitutions have plans that are used whether the pastor steps down in the wake of controversy, accepts a new pastorate or passes away, said Mims, former vice president of the church resources division of LifeWay Christian Resources of the Southern Baptist Convention.

"They will say language like, 'when the office is vacated' or 'when the pulpit is vacated,'" he said, adding that most will outline the process for establishing a search committee.

"Oftentimes, when a church like Judson is without a pastor for awhile, other pastors will have friends or colleagues whom they will recommend to the chairman of the search committee."

Larry Bridgesmith, an elder at Woodmont Hills, a Church of Christ congregation in south Nashville, said churches in his fellowship are autonomous; therefore, each has its own approach to developing a succession plan.

Five years ago, church elders approved a request by Rubel Shelly, Woodmont Hills' preaching minister, to share his preaching responsibilities with John York, a professor at Lipscomb University. Shelly, the church's preaching minister for 28 years, remains a member but now teaches on the weekends at Rochester College in Michigan, which members of the Churches of Christ opened in 1959 as North Central Christian College. York is lead speaker at Woodmont Hills, and others will assume pulpit roles periodically in the next year.

"When he decided to leave full-time ministry and go into full-time teaching, John was in place," Bridgesmith said. "This hasn't caused a major hiccup in the church. ...I think we are far better suited at Woodmont because of this exchange of the mantle. With John working alongside as Elisha did, there is an expectation that he has assumed some of the leadership roles. He's not an outsider and has been part of our community, our fellowship, for many years."

McClain said by working alongside his father, "change is gradual, almost seamless."

"He demonstrates wisdom to me. With my father, there are no big changes, just additions, and this has helped calm those who may have had issues."

When asked if he was ready to be an Elisha when his father asked him to work with him, McClain said, "No, I don't deserve it, but that is the flesh. But in the spirit, if he calls you, he equips you. The will of God will never take you anywhere the grace of God can't keep you."

Maintaining a Vision

The late Bishop Michael Lee Graves, founding pastor of The Temple Church in the Bordeaux neighborhood of Nashville, defined a ministerial succession plan similar to the Elijah/Elisha model that continues to inspire praise from local church leaders.

In December, the 57-year-old minister passed away after a bout with colon cancer. Before his death, he named long-time member and assistant minister the Rev. Darrell Drumwright, 30, as the person he wanted to continue the work of the 3,000-member congregation affiliated with the National Baptist Convention USA Inc. and the National Missionary Baptist Convention of America. Drumwright, a graduate of Tennessee State University and a 2000 graduate of Harvard Divinity School, is a faculty member at American Baptist College.

In the nine months since Graves' death, worship service attendance has been steady, with more than 300 new members joining the church. Church staff and volunteers maintain Graves' vision of being a "ministry that matters"—a phrase found on church literature - through various activities and programs for worshippers of all ages.

Ministers such as the Rev. Jerry Maynard II, pastor of operations at Cathedral of Praise in Nashville, applaud Graves' action.

"Many churches are started in disputes because there was confusion about who will lead after the pastor leaves or what direction will the church head," said Maynard, whose father, Bishop Jerry L. Maynard, is pastor of Cathedral of Praise, a Church of God in Christ congregation. "What he did was very visionary because there was little doubt about where the church was headed."

Graves established The Temple Church in 1977, and the first members were himself and his wife of 34 years, Eleanor

J. Newhouse Graves. Since then, the congregation has grown by several thousand and was once included in a Lilly Endowment-funded study about the nation's 300 outstanding Protestant churches.

"Whenever you follow a leader of the magnitude of Brother Graves or my father, you have huge shoes to fill," McClain said. "But God will provide for you and give you what you need. ...We should always be training an Elisha. If you noticed, Elisha followed Elijah around for a period of time, a period of learning. In every position that is held in the body of Christ, in every organization, you should be training someone to take your place and to pick up the mantle. If you don't, there will be a void in leadership."

Article published September 26, 2005 and used by permission of The Tennessean, *Nashville, Tennessee.*

Notes

_____

_____

_____

_____

_____

_____

_____

_____

_____

_____

_____

_____

BIBLIOGRAPHY

Brooks, Dr. George T. *Appendix V. Church Administrative Questionnaire.*

Chaucer, Geoffrey. *The Canterbury Tales: The Parson's Portrait.* Translated by Paul Halsall. Brooklyn: Fordham University, 1996. <http://www.fordham.edu/halsall/source/CT-prolog-para.html>

Kellar, M.Div., Mark S. *Service of Installation.* Jamaica: Reform Church of Jamaica.

Harbin, William J. *When a Pastor Leaves.* Brentwood: Church Ministers Information Department-The Tennessee Baptist Convention, 1987.

The Holy Bible. King James Version. Nashville: Thomas Nelson, Inc., 2001.

The Holy Bible. New International Version. New York: International Bible Society, 1984.